SOMERS LIBRARY

D1264711

Machines That Work

Big Loaders

Amy Hayes

Cavendish Square

New York

Published in 2016 by Cavendish Square Publishing, LLC
243 5th Avenue, Suite 136, New York, NY 10016

Copyright © 2016 by Cavendish Square Publishing, LLC

First Edition

No part of this publication may be reproduced, stored in a retrieval system, or transmitted in any form or by any means—electronic, mechanical, photocopying, recording, or otherwise—without the prior permission of the copyright owner. Request for permission should be addressed to Permissions, Cavendish Square Publishing, 243 5th Avenue, Suite 136, New York, NY 10016. Tel (877) 980-4450; fax (877) 980-4454.

Website: cavendishsq.com

This publication represents the opinions and views of the author based on his or her personal experience, knowledge, and research. The information in this book serves as a general guide only. The author and publisher have used their best efforts in preparing this book and disclaim liability rising directly or indirectly from the use and application of this book.

CPSIA Compliance Information: Batch #WS15CSQ

All websites were available and accurate when this book was sent to press.

Library of Congress Cataloging-in-Publication Data

Hayes, Amy, author.
Big loaders / Amy Hayes.
pages cm. — (Machines that work)
Includes index.
ISBN 978-1-50260-398-2 (hardcover) ISBN 978-1-50260-397-5 (paperback)
ISBN 978-1-50260-399-9 (ebook)
1. Loaders (Machines)—Juvenile literature. I. Title.

TL296.5.H39 2016
621.8'63—dc22

2015003086

Editorial Director: David McNamara
Copy Editor: Rebecca Rohan
Art Director: Jeffrey Talbot
Designer: Stephanie Flecha
Senior Production Manager: Jennifer Ryder-Talbot
Production Editor: Renni Johnson

The photographs in this book are used by permission and through the courtesy of: GeoStock/Getty Images, cover; velirina/Shutterstock.com, 5; lechatnoir/E+/Getty Images, 7; Sergey Malov/Shutterstock.com, 9; shaunl/E+/Getty Images, 11; Chris Sattlberger/Blend Images/Getty Images, 13; hsvrs/Vetta/Getty Images, 15; Leonard Zhukovsky/Shutterstock.com, 17; rtem/Shutterstock.com, 19; Four Oaks/Shutterstock.com, 21.

Printed in the United States of America

Contents

Loaders carry heavy things!

4

A loader has a long arm called a **boom**.

7

At the end of the boom is a **bucket**.

The bucket scoops up rocks and dirt.

11

Special loaders can carry heavy blocks.

13

Sometimes loaders work with
dump trucks.

They work on
construction sites.

16

17

Loaders move big things from one place to another.

19

Loaders are hard workers.

20

21

New Words

boom (BOOM) Part of the machine that acts like an arm.

bucket (BUK-it) An open container that is used to hold and carry things.

construction sites (con-STRUKT-shon SYTZ) Places where buildings are being built.

dump trucks (DUMP TRUKZ) A large truck that holds dirt and rocks that tilts to dump its contents.

Index

About the Author

Amy Hayes lives in the beautiful city of Buffalo, New York. She has written several books for children, including the Machines That Work and the Our Holidays series for Cavendish Square.

About BOOK WORMS

Bookworms help independent readers gain reading confidence through high-frequency words, simple sentences, and strong picture/text support. Each book explores a concept that helps children relate what they read to the world in which they live.

SOMERS LIBRARY